SINGIN' with the BIG BAND

11 standards for jazz vocalists

Volume I

How to Use This Book

Each arrangement has two CD tracks:

Demonstration track: The vocal part is *in* the mix. Listen to how the vocal part is performed by a professional vocalist for suggested phrasing, style and interpretation.

Sing-Along track: The vocal part has been taken ***out*** of the mix. ***You*** sing-along with the big band.

Featuring vocalist Paige Martin / The Belwin Jazz Big Band directed by Pete BarenBregge

alfred.com

ISBN-10: 0-7390-6519-X
ISBN-13: 978-0-7390-6519-8

NIGHT AND DAY

Words by Music by
COLE PORTER
Arranged by DAVE WOLPE

night and day.
Night and day,
under the hide of me.
There's an oh, such a hungry yearning burning inside of me.
And it's torment won't be through 'til you let me spend my life making love to you,
day and night, night and day.
To Coda
Ensemble
Sax Solo
Sax Solo
D.S. al Coda
Night and day
Coda
Night and day

JUST FRIENDS

Music by JOHN KLENNER
Lyric by SAM M. LEWIS
Arranged by DAVE WOLPE

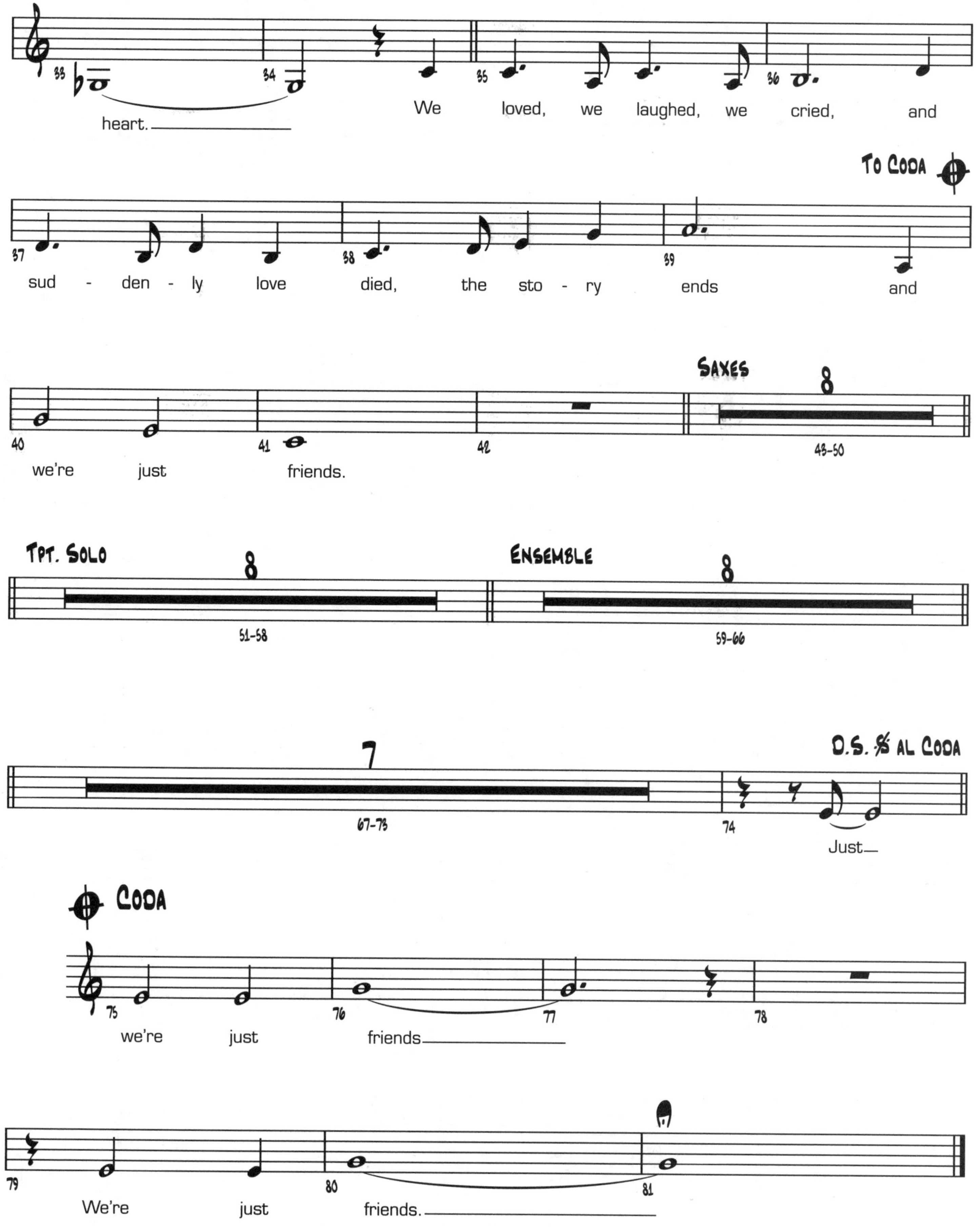
heart.
We loved, we laughed, we cried, and
To Coda
sud - den - ly love died, the sto - ry ends and
we're just friends.
Saxes
8
43-50
Tpt. Solo
8
51-58
Ensemble
8
59-66
7
67-73
D.S. al Coda
Just
Coda
we're just friends
We're just friends.

SOMETHING'S GOTTA GIVE

Words and Music by
JOHNNY MERCER
Arranged by DAVE WOLPE

45
46
47
48
from their vast my - ste - ri - ous sky?
I'll try hard
49
50
51
52
ig - nor - ing those lips I a - dore,
53
54
55
56
but how long can an - y - one try?
57
58
59
60
Fight, fight, fight, fight, fight it with all of our might,
61
62
63
64
chan - ces are some hea - ven - ly star - spang - led night,
TO CODA
65
66
67
68
we'll find out as sure as we live.
69
70
Some - thing's Got - ta Give, Some - thing's Got - ta Give, Some - thing's Got - ta
ENSEMBLE W/SAX SOLO
16
ENSEMBLE W/SAX SOLO
15
D.S. 𝄋 AL CODA
71
72
73-88
89-103
104
Give.
So, en - garde,
CODA
105
106
Some - thing's Got - ta Give, Some - thing's Got - ta Give,
107
108
109
Some - thing's Got - ta Give, Some - thing's Got - ta Give, Some - thing's Got - ta Give. Some - thing's
110
111
112
Got - ta Give. Some - thing's Got - ta Give.

SUMMER WIND

English Words by JOHNNY MERCER
Original German Lyrics by HANS BRADTKE
Music by HENRY MAYER
Arranged by DAVE WOLPE

34
35
I lost you to the sum - mer wind.
36
37
ENSEMBLE 8
SAX SOLO 7
38
39-46
47-53
54
The
55
au - tumn wind, the win - ter winds have come and gone,
56
57
58
59
60
and still the days, the lone - ly days go
61
62
63
on and on.
And guess who sighs his
64
65
66
lull - a - bies through nights that nev - er end,
67
68
69
70
my fick - le friend, the sum - mer wind.
71
72
73
My fick - le friend, the sum - mer wind, the
74
75
76
sum - mer wind,
the sum - mer wind.

EVERYTHING

Words and Music by MICHAEL BUBLE,
ALAN CHANG and AMY FOSTER
Arranged by W. SCOTT RAGSDALE

STRAIGHT EIGHTHS

You're a fal -
You're a car -

ling star, you're a get - a - way car, you're the line
ou - sel, you're a wish - ing well, and you light

in the sand when I go too far. You're the swim -
me up, when you ring my bell. You're a mys -

ming pool on an Aug - ust day, and you're the
ter - y, you're from out - er space, you're ev - ery

per - fect thing to say. And you play
min - ute of my ev - ery day. And I can't

it coy, but it's kind - da cute. Oh, when you
be - lieve, ah, that I'm your girl, Oh, when I

smile at me you know ex - act - ly what you do. Ba - by don't
get to kiss you, gee it puts me in a whirl. What - ev - er

pre - tend that you don't know it's true, 'cause you can
comes our way, oh, we'll see it thru, and you
see it when I look at you.
know that's what our love can do.
And in this cra - zy life,
and through these cra - zy times, it's you, it's you,
you make me sing, you're ev - ery line, you're ev - ery word,
you're Ev - ery - thing.
1.
2.
You're a car -
6
D♭/A♭ A♭
Bah dah bah
CMI7 F9 BMI7 E9 B♭MI7 A9
dah bah dop bop bah, bah bah dop bop bah.
A♭MAJ7 CMI7 F9 BMI7 E9
Bah dah bah dah bah dop bop bah,

B♭mi7
A9
A♭maj7
bah bah dop bop bah. And in this cra - zy life,
and through these cra - zy times, it's you, it's you,
you make me sing, you're ev - ery line, you're ev - ery word,
you're Ev - ery - thing. You're ev - ery
song, I sing a - long, 'cause you're my Ev - ery - thing.
2
Dmi7
G9
Bah dah bah dah bah dop bop bah,
D♭mi7
G♭9
Cmi7
B9
B♭maj7
bah bah dop bop bah. Bah dah bah
dah bah dop bop bah,
rit.
bah bah dop bop bah.

HOW ABOUT YOU?

Adapted from the New York Voices arrangement

I COULD WRITE A BOOK

DEMO 13 SING-ALONG 14

Words by LORENZ HART
Music by RICHARD RODGERS
Arranged by DARMON MEADER

MEDIUM SWING

3

1–3 4 5 6 7

p If they asked me I could write a book,

8 9 10 11 12 13

a - bout the way you walk and whis - per and look. I could write a

14 15 GLISS. 16 17 18 19

pre-face on how we met so the world would (n) ne - ver for - get

20 21 22 23 24 25 26

mf and the sim-ple sec-ret *mf* of the plot is just to tell them that I love you a - lot.

27 28 29 30 31 32

then the world dis - co-vers as my book ends, how to

33 34 35 36 37 38

make two lo - vers of friends. *mf* If they asked me I could

39 40 41 42 43

write a book a - bout the way, the way that you walk and whis - per and the way that you look

you a lot and then the world will dis - co - ver as my sto - ry ends
how to make two lo - vers of friends.
Ensemble
Tpt. Solo
Ensemble
Tpt. Solo
If they asked me I could write a book,
a - bout the way that you whis - per and walk and the way that you look.
I could write a pre - face on how we met so the
world world (n) ne - ver for - get and the
sim - ple sec - ret of the Per - fect plot is just to tell them that I love
you a - lot and the world will dis - co - ver as my fair - y tale ends how to make
two lov - ers out - ta two best friends how to make two lo - vers of two best friends,
how to make two lo - vers out - ta two best friends,
that's why I say I could write a book
(or tacet)
(improv. fill)

I'VE GOT YOU UNDER MY SKIN

Words and Music by
COLE PORTER
Arranged by DAVE WOLPE

41 sac - ri - fice an - y - thing, 42 come what might, for the 43 sake of hav - ing you
44 near. In spite of a 45 warn - ing voice that 46 comes in the night and re -
47 peats and re - peats in my 48 ear: "Don't you 49 know, lit - tle fool,
50 you ne - ver can 51 win. 52 Use your men - 53 tal - i - ty.
54 Wake up to re - 55 al - i - ty." 56 But each
57 time I do, just the 58 thought of you makes me 59 stop, be - fore I be -
To Coda
60 gin, 'cause I've 61 got you 62 un - der my
Ensemble 4
Tbn. Solo 8
Ensemble 7
D.S. al Coda
63 skin. 64 65-68 69-76 77-83 84 I
Coda
85 skin. 86 'cause I've 87 got you
88 un - der my 89 skin. 90 91

WHEN I FALL IN LOVE

Words by EDWARD HEYMAN
Music by VICTOR YOUNG
Arranged by DAVE WOLPE

heart. And the mo - ment I can feel that you
feel that way too, is when I fall in love with
you.
Ensemble
8
39-46
Tbn. Solo
8
47-54
When I give my heart
it will be com - plete - ly or I'll nev - er give my
heart. And the mo - ment I can feel that you
feel that way too, is when I fall in love with
Rit.
Slower
you. When I fall in love with you.
Rit.

I GET A KICK OUT OF YOU

Words by Music by
COLE PORTER
Arranged by DAVE WOLPE

stand - ing there be - fore me.
I get a kick tho' it's clear to me you
ob - vious - ly don't a - dore me.
I get no kick in a plane.
Fly - ing too high with some guy in the sky is my
To Coda
i - dea of noth - ing to do. Yet
I get a kick out of you.
Ensemble
16
71-86
Sax Solo
16
87-102
D.S. al Coda
Coda
I get a kick, yes! I get a
kick, yes! I get a kick out of you.

Adapted from the New York Voices arrangement

I CAN'T BELIEVE THAT YOU'RE IN LOVE WITH ME

Words and Music by
CLARENCE GASKILL and JIMMY McHUGH
Arranged by DARMON MEADER

42
they could do,
43
I can't be-lieve
44
that you're in love
45
with me.
46
So they say you're
47
tell - ing ev - 'ry
48
one I know
49
you're think - in' of me ev - 'ry
50
place you go
51
They can't be - lieve
52
you're in love with
53
me.
54
mf
I have al -
55
ways placed your en -
56
dear - ing face far a -
57
bove the reach of sim - ple
58
me.
I've been so
59
na - ive I can
60
hard - ly be - lieve
61
you've been think - in' of me,
62
mf
so that
63
now when all is said
64
an' done
who'd
65
ev - er thought we'd be the
66
luck - y ones?
67
I can't be - lieve
68
that you're in love with
69
me.
70
Ensemble w/Sax Solo
8
71-78
Ensemble w/Sax Solo
8
79-86
Sax Solo
8
87-94
Sax Solo
8
95-102
Optional Scat Line with Band (or Tacet)
103
Beh duh beh duh beh
104
deh yuh dow buh buh
105
duh beh ah buh deh buh duh dah

buh deh buh deh duht beh bah doo beh uh buh deh n deh ah
buh buh duh buh deh n beh n deh buhp bih uh buh duh beh y eh buh
deh buh doo doh buh beh buh duh beh ah buh deh buh deh doh
buh deh n duh deh n deh deh deh buhp deh bih di ya bah
doo beh ah m beh buh doo dle dih deh n doo weh yah daht
SUB. f
I have
al - ways placed you high a - bove the lone - ly crowd. I been so
na - ive, I can hard - ly be - lieve Oh, I'm gon - na sing it out loud, So that
now, when all is said an' done, who'd ev - er thought we'd be the
luck - y ones? I can't be-lieve that we're in love, Oh, you're the on - ly one I've been
think - in' of, I can't be - lieve, it's true that you've fall - en in love
with me.
mf
Ooo
RIT.
you're in love with me.